The *Everything* Binder *Book*

The *Everything* Binder *Book*

Financial, Estate, and Personal Affairs Organizer

Michelle Perry Higgins

Alive Book Publishing

The *Everything* Binder *Book*
Copyright © 2019 by Michelle Perry Higgins

All rights reserved. No part of this book may be reproduced or transmitted in any form or by any means without written permission from the publisher and author.

Additional copies may be ordered from the publisher for educational, business, promotional or premium use. For information, contact ALIVE Book Publishing at: alivebookpublishing.com, or call (925) 837-7303.

ISBN 13
978-1-63132-063-7

ISBN 10
1-63132-063-7

Library of Congress Control Number: 2019931324
Library of Congress Cataloging-in-Publication Data is available upon request.

First Edition

Published in the United States of America by ALIVE Book Publishing and
ALIVE Publishing Group, imprints of Advanced Publishing LLC
3200 A Danville Blvd., Suite 204, Alamo, California 94507
alivebookpublishing.com

PRINTED IN THE UNITED STATES OF AMERICA

10 9 8 7 6 5 4 3 2 1

The *Everything* Binder Book

Welcome

Life's pretty complicated these days. Over the years I've seen many of my clients struggle to find important information and documents when they really needed it. Fires, deaths, injuries, home sales, earthquakes, even weddings—you name it, there comes a time when all of us need to get our hands on some piece of important information for ourselves or for our loved ones.

The *Everything* Binder *Book* is an essential, easy-to-use system to organize all your important records and information. When an accident, illness or death occurs, your family and friends will turn to The *Everything* Binder *Book* for answers.

Assembling all your information can feel daunting, so I tell my clients to take it in small chunks. You'll be amazed at how fast it gets completed even if you only do a little on the weekends. From there it only gets easier, and before you know it, your information is up-to-date and in one safe place. The time you invest into this binder will alleviate the stress your loved ones will feel if anything happens to you unexpectedly.

Instructions for the owner(s) of this book:

1) Complete each section that applies to your situation.

2) Please notify at least two people (primary contacts) where and how to access this book. If you choose to do so, also show the contents of The *Everything* Binder *Book*. These individuals will access it in the event of illness or death.

3) Bring this book to the next meeting you have with your accountant, estate planner, financial planner and insurance agent. Review its contents and location to be stored with your professional team.

4) The book should be updated if any information changes; note any changes on the update log.

5) The *Everything* Binder *Book* should be stored in a secure location at all times.

Thanks for choosing The *Everything* Binder *Book* and becoming financially fit!

Michelle Higgins

Michelle Perry Higgins

IMPORTANT DISCLOSURE: *This is an organizational tool, not legal advice. Please consult a competent professional for advice in the areas of estate, insurance, tax and financial planning. This book is NOT a replacement for these services. The author and the publisher are not providing professional advice in any way but are instead providing an organizational tool for all your important personal information in the event of illness, incapacity or death. It is the book owner's responsibility to store this document in a secure location, in order to avoid risk of a security breach.*

Update Log

The *Everything* Binder last updated on: _____

Content changed: _____

My Signature: _____

Spouse/Partner Signature: _____

The *Everything* Binder last updated on: _____

Content changed: _____

My Signature: _____

Spouse/Partner Signature: _____

The *Everything* Binder last updated on: _____

Content changed: _____

My Signature: _____

Spouse/Partner Signature: _____

The *Everything* Binder last updated on: _____

Content changed: _____

My Signature: _____

Spouse/Partner Signature: _____

The *Everything* Binder last updated on: _____

Content changed: _____

My Signature: _____

Spouse/Partner Signature: _____

Table of Contents

- 11   Pre & Post-Death Checklists
- 15   Personal Information
  - Primary Contacts
  - My Information
  - Spouse/Partner Information
  - Children/Individuals Living in the Home
  - Others Who Rely on Me
- 23   Immediate Contacts
  - Professional Team
  - Doctors
  - Additional Contacts
- 31   Medical History
  - Personal Medical History
  - Spouse/Partner Medical History
  - Family Medical History
- 35   Insurance
  - Medical, Dental & Vision Insurance
  - Disability & Long Term Care Insurance
  - Home & Umbrella Insurance
  - Vehicle Insurance
  - Business Insurance
  - Life Insurance
  - Spouse/Partner Life Insurance
  - Other Insurance
- 47   Private Security & Access Information
  - Personal Devices
  - Business Devices
  - Miscellaneous Login Information
  - Spouse/Partner Personal Devices
  - Spouse/Partner Business Devices
  - Spouse/Partner Miscellaneous Login Information
- 55   Income & Cash Equivalents
  - Current Income Sources
  - Cash & Checking
  - Savings/Money Markets/CDs
  - Cash Loaned to Others
  - Safety Deposit Box
- 63   Real Estate
  - Primary & Secondary Residences
  - Other Property
- 67   Personal Property
  - Storage Unit & Safe
  - Vehicles
  - Art, Jewelry & Collections
  - Miscellaneous Personal Property
- 75   Retirement & Investments
  - Retirement Accounts
  - Pension & Social Security
  - Stock Options & Deferred Compensation Plan
  - Investment Accounts
  - Individual Stock Certificates & Bonds
  - Commodites, Savings Bonds & Annuities
  - Education & Other Accounts
  - Spouse/Partner Retirement Accounts
  - Spouse/Partner Pension & Social Security
  - Spouse/Partner Stock Options & Deferred Compensation Plan
  - Spouse/Partner Investment Accounts
  - Spouse/Partner Individual Stock Certificates & Bonds
  - Spouse/Partner Commodities, Savings Bonds & Annuities
  - Spouse/Partner Education & Other Accounts
- 91   Debt
  - Mortgages
  - Vehicle Loans
  - Student & Personal Loans
  - Credit Cards
  - Business & Other Debts
- 97   Business Ownership
  - Business Information
  - Important Business Documents
- 101   Document Originals & Copies
- 105   Four-Legged Friends
  - Pet Information
  - Livestock Information
- 109   Estate Planning Documents
  - Estate Plan Information
  - Spouse/Partner Estate Plan Information
- 113   Funeral Arrangements
  - Funeral Home & Cemetery Information
  - Cemetery Information & Organ Donation
  - Obituary
  - Funeral Service Details
  - Spouse/Partner Funeral Home & Cemetery Information
  - Spouse/Partner Cemetery Information & Organ Donation
  - Spouse/Partner Obituary
  - Spouse/Partner Funeral Service Details
- 131   Letters to Loved Ones

Pre & Post-Death Checklists

Pre & Post-Death Checklists

Accident/Illness Checklist	Date Completed	Person Spoken To
Call Emergency Contacts		
Arrange Care for Children		
Arrange Care for Others Who Rely on Me		
Arrange Care for Animals		
Review Income Sources		
Review Medical Benefits		
Review Health Care Insurance Policy		
Review Long Term Care Insurance Policy		
Review Disability Policy		
Review Medicare		
Review Union Benefits		
Contact Business Partner or Key Employee		
Contact Estate Planning Attorney		
Contact Financial Planner		
Contact Accountant		
Contact Spiritual Advisor		
Contact Employer Benefits Department		
Contact First Line Leader (Military)		
Manage Residence Maintenance		
Manage Residence Utilities		
Maintain Payment of All Bills		
Pick Up Mail		
Manage Pool		
Manage Gardener		
Manage Cleaner		
Check Email Accounts/Other Sites		

Pre & Post-Death Checklists

Post-Death Checklist	Date Completed	Person Spoken To
Arrange Organ Donation		
Arrange Care for Children		
Arrange Care for Others Who Rely on Me		
Arrange Care for Animals		
Plan Funeral Arrangements		
Plan Reception Arrangements		
Contact Friends and Family		
Write and Publish Obituary		
Obtain Death Certificates (12-15 copies)		
Contact Estate Planning Attorney		
Contact Financial Planner		
Review Retirement Accounts		
Review Investment Accounts		
Change of Beneficiary Forms Retirement Plans		
Change of Beneficiary Forms Other Accounts		
Contact Accountant		
Contact Spiritual Advisor		
Contact Property & Casualty Insurance Agent		
Contact Life Insurance Companies		
Contact Employer Benefits Life Insurance		
Contact Employer Benefits Retirement Plans		
Contact Employer Benefits Medical		
Contact Employer Benefits Other		
Contact First Line Leader (Military)		
Empty Storage Unit		
Empty Safe Contents		
Empty Safe Deposit Box		
Contact Medicare		
Contact Social Security		
Contact Union Benefits		
Contact Post Office		
Real Estate Affairs Primary Residence		
Real Estate Affairs Other Property		
Contact Credit Card Companies		
Contact Student Loan Companies		
Contact Business Partner or Key Employee		
Close Memberships		
Close Social Media Accounts		
Close Email Accounts/Other Sites		
Cancel All Home Deliveries		

Personal Information

Personal Information

Primary Contacts

Individuals to Contact in the Event of Accident, Illness or Death

Name _____

Address _____

Phone _____

Email _____

Relationship _____

Individual knows about this binder [choose one]   ○ yes ○ no

Reviewed content of this binder [choose one]   ○ yes ○ no

Name _____

Address _____

Phone _____

Email _____

Relationship _____

Individual knows about this binder [choose one]   ○ yes ○ no

Reviewed content of this binder [choose one]   ○ yes ○ no

Personal Information

My Information

My Name (Legal Name) _____

Other Known Name(s) _____

Address _____

Alarm Code to Enter Home _____

Alarm Company Passcode (if applicable) _____

P.O. Box _____

Location of P.O. Box _____

Social Security Number _____

Location of Social Security Card _____

Date of Birth _____

Citizenship (Country) _____

Phone _____

Email _____

Employer Name _____

Job Title _____

Address _____

Phone _____

Date of Hire _____

Name of Supervisor _____

Supervisor Phone _____

Military Service (Branch & Status) _____

First Line Supervisor _____

Phone _____

Email _____

Commanding Officer _____

Phone _____

Email _____

Personal Information

Spouse/Partner Information

Name of Spouse/Partner (Legal Name) _____

Other Known Name(s) _____

Address _____

Alarm Code to Enter Home _____

P.O. Box _____

Location of P.O. Box _____

Social Security Number _____

Location of Social Security Card _____

Date of Birth _____

Citizenship (Country) _____

Phone _____

Email _____

Spouse/Partner's Employer Name _____

Job Title _____

Address _____

Phone _____

Date of Hire _____

Name of Supervisor _____

Supervisor Phone _____

Spouse/Partner's Military Service (Branch & Status) _____

First Line Supervisor _____

Phone _____

Email _____

Commanding Officer _____

Phone _____

Email _____

Personal Information

Children/Individuals Living in the Home

Full Name _____

Phone Number _____

Date of Birth _____

Relationship to You _____

Social Security Number _____

Location of Social Security Card _____

Grade _____

Trusted Friends _____

Things I must know about your child

```
┌─────────────────────────────────────────────┐
│                                             │
│                                             │
└─────────────────────────────────────────────┘
```

My Child's School/Daycare Information

Name of School/Daycare _____

Contact at School/Daycare _____

Phone _____

Cell Phone _____

Email _____

Other _____

Individuals authorized to pick up children from school or daycare

```
┌─────────────────────────────────────────────┐
│                                             │
│                                             │
└─────────────────────────────────────────────┘
```

Family Code Word _____

Personal Information

Children/Individuals Living in the Home

Full Name
Phone Number
Date of Birth
Relationship to You
Social Security Number
Location of Social Security Card
Grade
Trusted Friends
Things I must know about your child

My Child's School/Daycare Information

Name of School/Daycare
Contact at School/Daycare
Phone
Cell Phone
Email
Other

Individuals authorized to pick up children from school or daycare

Family Code Word

Personal Information

Others Who Rely on Me

Others Who Rely on Me

Name
Phone
Cell Phone
Email
Important care instructions

Name
Phone
Cell Phone
Email
Important care instructions

Name
Phone
Cell Phone
Email
Important care instructions

Name
Phone
Cell Phone
Email
Important care instructions

Name
Phone
Cell Phone
Email
Important care instructions

Immediate Contacts

Immediate Contacts

Professional Team

Accountant

Full Name

Company/Firm

Address

Phone

Email

This accountant completed my tax return ◯ yes ◯ no

I/We complete our own tax return ◯ yes ◯ no

Additional Information

Attorney

Full Name

Company/Firm

Type of Attorney

Address

Phone

Email

Additional Information

Financial Planner

Full Name

Company/Firm

Address

Phone

Email

Additional Information

Immediate Contacts
Professional Team

Insurance Agent (Property & Casualty)

Full Name

Company/Firm

Address

Phone

Email

Additional Information

Insurance Agent (Life)

Full Name

Company/Firm

Address

Phone

Email

Additional Information

Real Estate Agent

Full Name

Company/Firm

Address

Phone

Email

Additional Information

Immediate Contacts

Doctors

Physician

Full Name
Address
Phone
Email
Additional Information

Pediatrician

Full Name
Address
Phone
Email
Additional Information

Optometrist/Ophthalmologist

Full Name
Address
Phone
Email
Additional Information

Dentist

Full Name
Address
Phone
Email
Additional Information

Immediate Contacts *Doctors*

Veterinarian

Full Name

Address

Phone

Email

Additional Information

Other Doctor

Full Name

Address

Phone

Email

Additional Information

Preferred Hospital

Full Name

Address

Phone

Additional Information

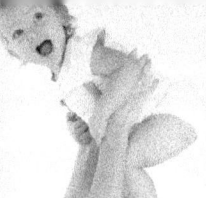

Immediate Contacts

Additional Contacts

Religious Affiliation

Full Name

Address

Phone

Email

Additional Information

Other

Full Name

Address

Phone

Email

Additional Information

Other

Full Name

Address

Phone

Email

Additional Information

Other

Full Name

Address

Phone

Email

Additional Information

Immediate Contacts

Additional Contacts

Name	Company	Phone
Water		
Electricity		
Home Alarm Service		
Sanitation		
Telephone		
Internet		
Oil/Gas		
Gardener		
Handyman		
Pool Service		
Home Cleaner		
Property Manager		
Plumber		
Electrician		
Maintenance		
Programs		
Subscriptions		
Memberships		
Charity		
Other		
Other		
Other		
Other		

Any important notes to this section:

Medical History

Medical History

Personal Medical History

My Name

Past Surgeries and Dates

Current medical conditions

Current medications

Dosage of medications

Frequency of medication

Allergies to medicine/food

Blood type

Do you have any health problems?

Additional health information

Important family medical history

Medical History

Spouse/Partner Medical History

Spouse/Partner Name

Past Surgeries and Dates

Current medical conditions

Current medications

Dosage of medications

Frequency of medication

Allergies to medicine/food

Blood type

Do you have any health problems?

Additional health information

Important family medical history

Medical History

Family Medical History

Children/Individuals Living in the Home

Name

Past Surgeries & Dates

Current medical conditions

Current medication

Dosage of medication

Frequency of medication

Allergies to medicine/food

Blood type

Do you have any health problems?

Additional health information

Important family medical history

Children/Individuals Living in the Home

Name

Past Surgeries & Dates

Current medical conditions

Current medication

Dosage of medication

Frequency of medication

Allergies to medicine/food

Blood type

Do you have any health problems?

Additional health information

Important family medical history

Insurance

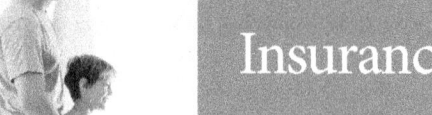

Insurance

Medical, Dental & Vision Insurance

Medical Insurance

Employer Group or Individual Plan

Employer Name

Medical Insurance Provider

Phone

Policy Number

Policy covers the following people

Website

Username

Password

Dental Insurance

Employer Group or Individual Plan

Employer Name

Dental Insurance Provider

Phone

Policy Number

Policy covers the following people

Website

Username

Password

Vision Insurance

Employer Group or Individual Plan

Employer Name

Vision Insurance Provider

Phone

Policy Number

Policy covers the following people

Website

Username

Password

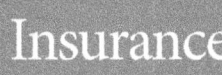

Insurance

Disability & Long Term Care Insurance

Disability Insurance

Employer Group or Individual Plan

Employer Name

Disability Insurance Provider

Phone

Policy Number

Policy covers the following people

Website

Username

Password

Long Term Care Insurance

Employer Group or Individual Plan

Employer Name

Long Term Care Insurance Provider

Phone

Policy Number

Policy covers the following people

Website

Username

Password

Insurance

Home Insurance

Primary Residence - Homeowner's Insurance

Property Address
Company Name
Agent Name
Phone
Holder Name
Policy Number
Location of Policy
Website
Username   Password

Renter's Insurance

Property Address
Company Name
Agent Name
Phone
Holder Name
Policy Number
Location of Policy
Website
Username   Password

Other Property - Homeowner's Insurance

Property Address
Company Name
Agent Name
Phone
Holder Name
Policy Number
Location of Policy
Website
Username   Password

Insurance

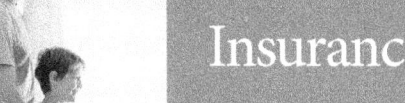

Home & Umbrella Insurance

Other Property - Homeowner's Insurance

Property Address

Company Name

Agent Name

Phone

Holder Name

Policy Number

Location of Policy

Website

Username

Password

Umbrella Insurance

Company Name

Agent Name

Phone

Holder Name

Policy Number

Location of Policy

Website

Username

Password

Insurance

Vehicle Insurance

Select One

☐ Auto ☐ Boat ☐ RV ☐ Motorcycle ☐ Other

Make/Model/Year

VIN #

Company Name

Agent Name

Phone

Holder Name

Policy Number

Location of Policy

Website

Username

Password

☐ Auto ☐ Boat ☐ RV ☐ Motorcycle ☐ Other

Make/Model/Year

VIN #

Company Name

Agent Name

Phone

Holder Name

Policy Number

Location of Policy

Website

Username

Password

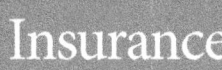

Insurance

Vehicle Insurance

Select One

☐ Auto ☐ Boat ☐ RV ☐ Motorcycle ☐ Other

Make/Model/Year _____

VIN # _____

Company Name _____

Agent Name _____

Phone _____

Holder Name _____

Policy Number _____

Location of Policy _____

Website _____

Username _____

Password _____

☐ Auto ☐ Boat ☐ RV ☐ Motorcycle ☐ Other

Make/Model/Year _____

VIN # _____

Company Name _____

Agent Name _____

Phone _____

Holder Name _____

Policy Number _____

Location of Policy _____

Website _____

Username _____

Password _____

Insurance

Business Insurance

Company Name

Agent Name

Phone

Holder Name

Policy Number

Location of Policy

Website

Username

Password

Secondary Business Insurance

Company Name

Agent Name

Phone

Holder Name

Policy Number

Location of Policy

Website

Username

Password

Insurance

Life Insurance

Myself

My Name
Type of Life Insurance
Person Covered
Death Benefit
Cash Value
Primary Beneficiary
Contingent Beneficiary
Company Name
Agent Name
Phone
Policy Number
Location of Policy
Website
Username
Password

Type of Life Insurance
Person Covered
Death Benefit
Cash Value
Primary Beneficiary
Contingent Beneficiary
Company Name
Agent Name
Phone
Policy Number
Location of Policy
Website
Username
Password

Insurance

Life Insurance

Spouse/Partner

Spouse/Partner Name
Type of Life Insurance
Person Covered
Death Benefit
Cash Value
Primary Beneficiary
Contingent Beneficiary
Company Name
Agent Name
Phone
Policy Number
Location of Policy
Website
Username
Password

Type of Life Insurance
Person Covered
Death Benefit
Cash Value
Primary Beneficiary
Contingent Beneficiary
Company Name
Agent Name
Phone
Policy Number
Location of Policy
Website
Username
Password

Insurance

Other Insurance

Describe Asset
Company Name
Agent Name
Phone
Holder Name
Policy Number
Location of Policy
Website
Username   Password

Describe Asset
Company Name
Agent Name
Phone
Holder Name
Policy Number
Location of Policy
Website
Username   Password

Describe Asset
Company Name
Agent Name
Phone
Holder Name
Policy Number
Location of Policy
Website
Username   Password

Private Security & Access Information

Private Security & Access Information

Personal Devices

Myself

Personal Security/Access Information

My Name

Personal Cellular Phone

Personal Cellular Phone Number

Password to Unlock

Provider

Notes

Personal Laptop

Personal Laptop Password to Open

Important Documents

People who access this computer

Notes

Personal Computer

Personal Computer Password to Open

Important Documents

People who access this computer

Notes

Personal iPad or Tablet

Personal iPad or Tablet Password to Open

Important Documents

People who access this computer

Notes

Other Personal Device

Password to Open

Important Documents

People who access this device

Notes

Private Security & Access Information

Business Devices

Myself

Business Security/Access Information

Business Cellular Phone _____

Business Cellular Phone Number _____

Password to Unlock _____

Provider _____

Notes _____

Business Laptop

Business Laptop Password to Open _____

Important Documents _____

People who access this computer _____

Notes _____

Business Computer

Business Computer Password to Open _____

Important Documents _____

People who access this computer _____

Notes _____

Business iPad or Tablet

Business iPad or Tablet Password to Open _____

Important Documents _____

People who access this computer _____

Notes _____

Other Business Device

Password to Open _____

Important Documents _____

People who access this device _____

Notes _____

Private Security & Access Information

Miscellaneous Login Information

Myself

My Name
Personal Fax Number
Notes

Business Fax Number
Notes

Facebook
User Name
Password

Twitter
User Name
Password

Google+
User Name
Password

Other
User Name
Password

Email #1
User Name
Password

Email #2
User Name
Password

Email #3
User Name
Password

Skype
User Name
Password

Apple
Apple ID
Password

Storage Online
URL
User Name
Password

Photo Storage
URL
User Name
Password

Subscriptions
URL
User Name
Password

Games
URL
User Name
Password

Other
URL
User Name
Password

Private Security & Access Information

Personal Devices

Spouse/Partner

Personal Security/Access Information

Spouse/Partner Name

Personal Cellular Phone

Personal Cellular Phone Number

Password to Unlock

Provider

Notes

Personal Laptop

Personal Laptop Password to Open

Important Documents

People who access this computer

Notes

Personal Computer

Personal Computer Password to Open

Important Documents

People who access this computer

Notes

Personal iPad or Tablet

Personal iPad or Tablet Password to Open

Important Documents

People who access this computer

Notes

Other Personal Device

Password to Open

Important Documents

People who access this device

Notes

Private Security & Access Information

Business Devices

Spouse/Partner

Business Security/Access Information

Business Cellular Phone _____

Business Cellular Phone Number _____

Password to Unlock _____

Provider _____

Notes _____

Business Laptop

Business Laptop Password to Open _____

Important Documents _____

People who access this computer _____

Notes _____

Business Computer

Business Computer Password to Open _____

Important Documents _____

People who access this computer _____

Notes _____

Business iPad or Tablet

Business iPad or Tablet Password to Open _____

Important Documents _____

People who access this computer _____

Notes _____

Other Business Device

Password to Open _____

Important Documents _____

People who access this device _____

Notes _____

Private Security & Access Information

Miscellaneous Login Information

Spouse/Partner

Spouse/Partner Name
Personal Fax Number
Notes

Business Fax Number
Notes

Facebook
User Name
Password

Twitter
User Name
Password

Google+
User Name
Password

Other
User Name
Password

Email #1
User Name
Password

Email #2
User Name
Password

Email #3
User Name
Password

Skype
User Name
Password

Apple
Apple ID
Password

Storage Online
URL
User Name
Password

Photo Storage
URL
User Name
Password

Subscriptions
URL
User Name
Password

Games
URL
User Name
Password

Other
URL
User Name
Password

Income & Cash Equivalents

Income & Cash Equivalents

Current Income Sources

	My Monthly or Annual	Spouse/Partner Monthly or Annual
Salary		
Bonus		
Self Employed		
IRA Distributions		
Interest & Dividends		
Business		
Alimony		
Child Support		
Disability		
Social Security		
Unemployment		
Pension		
Other		
TOTAL		

Provide copies of statements.

Any important notes to this section: _____

Income & Cash Equivalents

Cash & Checking

Cash in Home

Location

Amount

Checking Account

Name(s) on Account

Name of Bank

Account Number

Address

Phone

Website

Username

Password

Debit Card

Bills are paid out of this account   ○ yes   ○ no

Bills paid online   ○ yes   ○ no

Bills automatically drafted? *If yes, please attach list*   ○ yes   ○ no

Bills paid with checks   ○ yes   ○ no

If yes, checks are located

Checking Account

Name(s) on Account

Name of Bank

Account Number

Address

Phone

Website

Username

Password

Debit Card

Bills are paid out of this account   ○ yes   ○ no

Bills paid online   ○ yes   ○ no

Bills automatically drafted? *If yes, please attach list*   ○ yes   ○ no

Bills paid with checks   ○ yes   ○ no

If yes, checks are located

Income & Cash Equivalents

Savings/Money Markets/CDs

Savings Accounts/Money Markets/CDs

Name(s) on Account

Name of Bank

Account Number

Type of Account

Address

Phone

Website

Username

Password

Additional Accounts at this Bank

Name(s) on Account

Account Number

Type of Account

Additional Accounts at this Bank

Name(s) on Account

Account Number

Type of Account

Additional Accounts at this Bank

Name(s) on Account

Account Number

Type of Account

Additional Accounts at this Bank

Name(s) on Account

Account Number

Type of Account

Income & Cash Equivalents

Savings/Money Markets/CDs

Savings Accounts/Money Markets/CDs

Name(s) on Account

Name of Bank

Account Number

Type of Account

Address

Phone

Website

Username

Password

Additional Accounts at this Bank

Name(s) on Account

Account Number

Type of Account

Additional Accounts at this Bank

Name(s) on Account

Account Number

Type of Account

Additional Accounts at this Bank

Name(s) on Account

Account Number

Type of Account

Additional Accounts at this Bank

Name(s) on Account

Account Number

Type of Account

Income & Cash Equivalents

Cash Loaned to Others

Cash Loaned to Others

Person who owes me money _____

Amount _____

Terms of Loan (interest, length, payment) _____

Loan Documentation _____

Upon death, loan is forgiven   ○ yes   ○ no

Notes _____

Person who owes me money _____

Amount _____

Terms of Loan (interest, length, payment) _____

Loan Documentation _____

Upon death, loan is forgiven   ○ yes   ○ no

Notes _____

Person who owes me money _____

Amount _____

Terms of Loan (interest, length, payment) _____

Loan Documentation _____

Upon death, loan is forgiven   ○ yes   ○ no

Notes _____

Person who owes me money _____

Amount _____

Terms of Loan (interest, length, payment) _____

Loan Documentation _____

Upon death, loan is forgiven   ○ yes   ○ no

Notes _____

Income & Cash Equivalents

Safety Deposit Box

Safety Deposit Box Inventory

Name of Bank

Box Number

Address

Phone

Authorized Signers

Location of Key

List of Safety Deposit Box Content

1.
2.
3.
4.
5.
6.
7.
8.
9.
10.
11.
12.
13.
14.
15.

Any important notes to this section:

Real Estate

Real Estate
Primary & Secondary Residences

Primary Residence

Address

Owner(s)

Percentage Ownership

Estimated Property Value

Purchase Price and Date

Annual Property Tax

Deed Location

Photos of property are included in binder   ◯ yes ◯ no

Special Instructions for Property

Secondary Residence

Address

Owner(s)

Percentage Ownership

Estimated Property Value

Purchase Price and Date

Annual Property Tax

Deed Location

Photos of property are included in binder   ◯ yes ◯ no

Special Instructions for Property

Real Estate

Other Property

Other Property

Address

Owner(s)

Percentage Ownership

Estimated Property Value

Purchase Price and Date

Annual Property Tax

Deed Location

Photos of property are included in binder ⚪ yes ⚪ no

Special Instructions for Property

Other Property

Address

Owner(s)

Percentage Ownership

Estimated Property Value

Purchase Price and Date

Annual Property Tax

Deed Location

Photos of property are included in binder ⚪ yes ⚪ no

Special Instructions for Property

Any important notes to this section:

Personal Property

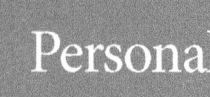

Personal Property

Storage Unit & Safe

Storage Unit

Storage Name _____

Address _____

Phone _____

Location of Key _____

Storage Number _____

Who else has access to storage unit? _____

Photos of content in storage unit?   ◯ yes ◯ no

Notes _____

Attach Inventory List

Safe

Key or Code _____

Key Location _____

Location of Safe _____

Who else has code or key? _____

Photos of content in the safe?   ◯ yes ◯ no

Notes _____

Attach Inventory List

Personal Property

Vehicles

Select One

☐ Auto   ☐ Boat   ☐ RV   ☐ Motorcycle   ☐ Other

Make/Model/Year

Own/Lease

Approximate Value

Storage Location

Location of Extra Keys

Location of Records

Photos   ◯ yes ◯ no

Best Source of Liquidation

Notes

☐ Auto   ☐ Boat   ☐ RV   ☐ Motorcycle   ☐ Other

Make/Model/Year

Own/Lease

Approximate Value

Storage Location

Location of Extra Keys

Location of Records

Photos   ◯ yes ◯ no

Best Source of Liquidation

Notes

☐ Auto   ☐ Boat   ☐ RV   ☐ Motorcycle   ☐ Other

Make/Model/Year

Own/Lease

Approximate Value

Storage Location

Location of Extra Keys

Location of Records

Photos   ◯ yes ◯ no

Best Source of Liquidation

Notes

Personal Property

Art, Jewlery & Collections

Art

Artist/Art Description

Estimated Value

Appraisal   ○ yes ○ no

Photos   ○ yes ○ no

Best Source of Liquidation

Notes

Attach Inventory List

Jewelry

Manufacturer/Jewelry Description

Estimated Value

Appraisal   ○ yes ○ no

Photos   ○ yes ○ no

Best Source of Liquidation

Notes

Attach Inventory List

Collections

Manufacturer/Model

Estimated Value

Appraisal   ○ yes ○ no

Photos   ○ yes ○ no

Best Source of Liquidation

Notes

Attach Inventory List

Personal Property

Art, Jewlery & Collections

Antiques

Manufacturer/Model

Estimated Value

Appraisal   ○ yes ○ no

Photos   ○ yes ○ no

Best Source of Liquidation

Notes

Attach Inventory List

Musical Instruments

Manufacturer/Model

Estimated Value

Appraisal   ○ yes ○ no

Photos   ○ yes ○ no

Best Source of Liquidation

Notes

Attach Inventory List

Personal Property

Miscellaneous Personal Property

Farm & Landscape Equipment

Manufacturer/Model

Estimated Value

Appraisal   ○ yes ○ no

Photos   ○ yes ○ no

Best Source of Liquidation

Notes

Attach Inventory List

Manufacturer/Model

Estimated Value

Appraisal   ○ yes ○ no

Photos   ○ yes ○ no

Best Source of Liquidation

Notes

Attach Inventory List

Manufacturer/Model

Estimated Value

Appraisal   ○ yes ○ no

Photos   ○ yes ○ no

Best Source of Liquidation

Notes

Attach Inventory List

Manufacturer/Model

Estimated Value

Appraisal   ○ yes ○ no

Photos   ○ yes ○ no

Best Source of Liquidation

Notes

Attach Inventory List

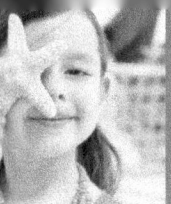

Personal Property

Miscellaneous Personal Property

Firearms

Manufacturer/Model

Serial #

Estimated Value

Appraisal   ○ yes ○ no

Photos   ○ yes ○ no

Gun Safe Key or Code

Best Source of Liquidation

Notes

Attach Inventory List

Other

Manufacturer/Model

Estimated Value

Appraisal   ○ yes ○ no

Photos   ○ yes ○ no

Notes

Other

Manufacturer/Model

Estimated Value

Appraisal   ○ yes ○ no

Photos   ○ yes ○ no

Notes

Other

Manufacturer/Model

Estimated Value

Appraisal   ○ yes ○ no

Photos   ○ yes ○ no

Notes

Retirement & Investments

Retirement & Investments

Retirement Accounts

Myself

Retirement Account

My Name

Type of Account

Name of Custodian

Financial Planner

Phone

Account Number

Website

Username

Password

Statement Located

Primary Beneficiary

Contingent Beneficiary

Retirement Account

My Name

Type of Account

Name of Custodian

Financial Planner

Phone

Account Number

Website

Username

Password

Statement Located

Primary Beneficiary

Contingent Beneficiary

Retirement & Investments

Pension & Social Security

Myself

Pension

Employer Name

Phone

Monthly Benefit

Start Date

Survivor Monthly Benefits

Survivor Lump Sum Benefit

Statement Located

Employer Name

Phone

Monthly Benefit

Start Date

Survivor Monthly Benefits

Survivor Lump Sum Benefit

Statement Located

Employer Name

Phone

Monthly Benefit

Start Date

Survivor Monthly Benefits

Survivor Lump Sum Benefit

Statement Located

Social Security

Full Benefit Amount

Statement Located

Retirement & Investments

Stock Options & Deferred Compensation Plan

Myself

Stock Options

Name and Ticker of Stock
Type of Stock Options
Name of Custodian
Phone
Account Number
Website
Username
Password
Statement Located

Stock Savings Plan

Name and Ticker of Stock
Name of Custodian
Phone
Account Number
Website
Username
Statement Located

Deferred Compensation Plan

Employer Name
Name of Custodian
Phone
Account Number
Website
Username
Password
Statement Located

Retirement & Investments

Investment Accounts

Myself

Investment Account

Type of Account

Name(s) on Account

Name of Custodian

Financial Planner

Phone

Account Number

Website

Username

Password

Statement Located

Investment Account

Type of Account

Name(s) on Account

Name of Custodian

Financial Planner

Phone

Account Number

Website

Username

Password

Statement Located

Retirement & Investments

Individual Stock Certificates & Bonds

Myself

Individual Stock Certificate

Stock Name & Ticker

Number of Shares

Certificate Located

Individual Stock Certificate

Stock Name & Ticker

Number of Shares

Certificate Located

Individual Bond

Type of Bond

Name of Bond

Face Amount

Maturity Date

Bond Located

Individual Bond

Type of Bond

Name of Bond

Face Amount

Maturity Date

Bond Located

Retirement & Investments

Commodities, Savings Bonds & Annuities

Myself

Commodity

Type of Commodity

Estimated Value

Commodity Located

Savings Bond

Type of Savings Bond

Name on Account

Estimated Value

Savings Bond Located

Annuity

Annuity Company

Fixed or Variable

Financial Planner

Phone

Account Number

Website

Username

Password

Primary Beneficiary

Contingent Beneficiary

Statement Located

Retirement & Investments

Education & Other Accounts

Myself

Education Account

Type of Account
Owner
Beneficiary (child)
Name of Custodian
Financial Planner
Phone
Account Number
Website
Username
Password
Statement Located

Other Account

Type of Account
Name(s) on Account
Name of Custodian
Financial Planner
Phone
Account Number
Website
Username
Password
Statement Located

Retirement & Investments

Retirement Accounts

Spouse/Partner

Retirement Account

Spouse/Partner Name

Type of Account

Name of Custodian

Financial Planner

Phone

Account Number

Website

Username

Password

Statement Located

Primary Beneficiary

Contingent Beneficiary

Retirement Account

Spouse/Partner Name

Type of Account

Name of Custodian

Financial Planner

Phone

Account Number

Website

Username

Password

Statement Located

Primary Beneficiary

Contingent Beneficiary

Retirement & Investments

Pension & Social Security

Spouse/Partner

Pension

Employer Name

Phone

Monthly Benefit

Start Date

Survivor Monthly Benefits

Survivor Lump Sum Benefit

Statement Located

Employer Name

Phone

Monthly Benefit

Start Date

Survivor Monthly Benefits

Survivor Lump Sum Benefit

Statement Located

Employer Name

Phone

Monthly Benefit

Start Date

Survivor Monthly Benefits

Survivor Lump Sum Benefit

Statement Located

Social Security

Full Benefit Amount

Statement Located

Retirement & Investments

Stock Options & Deferred Compensation Plan

Spouse/Partner

Stock Options

Name and Ticker of Stock

Type of Stock Options

Name of Custodian

Phone

Account Number

Website

Username

Password

Statement Located

Stock Savings Plan

Name and Ticker of Stock

Name of Custodian

Phone

Account Number

Website

Username

Statement Located

Deferred Compensation Plan

Employer Name

Name of Custodian

Phone

Account Number

Website

Username

Password

Statement Located

Retirement & Investments

Investment Accounts

Spouse/Partner

Investment Account

Type of Account

Name(s) on Account

Name of Custodian

Financial Planner

Phone

Account Number

Website

Username

Password

Statement Located

Investment Account

Type of Account

Name(s) on Account

Name of Custodian

Financial Planner

Phone

Account Number

Website

Username

Password

Statement Located

Retirement & Investments

Individual Stock Certificates & Bonds

Spouse/Partner

Individual Stock Certificate

Stock Name & Ticker

Number of Shares

Certificate Located

Individual Stock Certificate

Stock Name & Ticker

Number of Shares

Certificate Located

Individual Bond

Type of Bond

Name of Bond

Face Amount

Maturity Date

Bond Located

Individual Bond

Type of Bond

Name of Bond

Face Amount

Maturity Date

Bond Located

Retirement & Investments

Commodities, Savings Bonds & Annuities

Spouse/Partner

Commodity

Type of Commodity

Estimated Value

Commodity Located

Savings Bond

Type of Savings Bond

Name on Account

Estimated Value

Savings Bond Located

Annuity

Annuity Company

Fixed or Variable

Financial Planner

Phone

Account Number

Website

Username

Password

Primary Beneficiary

Contingent Beneficiary

Statement Located

Retirement & Investments

Education & Other Accounts

Spouse/Partner

Education Account

Type of Account
Owner
Beneficiary (*child*)
Name of Custodian
Financial Planner
Phone
Account Number
Website
Username
Password
Statement Located

Other Account

Type of Account
Name(s) on Account
Name of Custodian
Financial Planner
Phone
Account Number
Website
Username
Password
Statement Located

Any important notes to this section:

Debt

Debt

Mortgages

Address of Mortgage

Type of Property

Name(s) on Loan

Type of Loan (1st, 2nd, HEL)

Lender

Account Number

Mortgage Amount

Terms of Loan (interest, length, payment)

Lender Phone

Website

Username

Password

Location of Records

Address of Mortgage

Type of Property

Name(s) on Loan

Type of Loan (1st, 2nd, HEL)

Lender

Account Number

Mortgage Amount

Terms of Loan (interest, length, payment)

Lender Phone

Website

Username

Password

Location of Records

Debt

Vehicle Loans

Vehicle Loans

Make/Model/Year

Name(s) on Loan

Lender

Account Number

Loan Amount

Terms of Loan (interest, length, payment)

Lender Phone

Website

Username

Password

Location of Records

Make/Model/Year

Name(s) on Loan

Lender

Account Number

Loan Amount

Terms of Loan (interest, length, payment)

Lender Phone

Website

Username

Password

Location of Records

Debt

Student & Personal Loans

Student Loan

Name(s) on Loan

Lender

Account Number

Loan Amount

Terms of Loan (interest, length, payment)

Lender Phone

Website

Username

Password

Location of Records

Personal Loan (Due to Family/Friend)

Lender

Phone Number

Email

Amount Owed

Terms of Loan (interest, length, payment)

Loan Documentation

Upon death, loan is forgiven ◯ yes ◯ no

Debt

Credit Cards

Credit Card

Name of Company

Card Number

Amount Owed

Phone

Website

Username

Password

Credit Card

Name of Company

Card Number

Amount Owed

Phone

Website

Username

Password

Credit Card

Name of Company

Card Number

Amount Owed

Phone

Website

Username

Password

Debt

Business & Other Debts

Business Debt

Name(s) on Loan

Type of Loan (1st, 2nd, HEL)

Lender

Account Number

Mortgage Amount

Terms of Loan (interest, length, payment)

Lender Phone

Website

Username

Password

Location of Record

Other Debt

Name(s) on Loan

Type of Loan (1st, 2nd, HEL)

Lender

Account Number

Mortgage Amount

Terms of Loan (interest, length, payment)

Lender Phone

Website

Username

Password

Location of Record

Business Ownership

Business Ownership

Business Information

Name of Business
Type of Business
Ownership Percentage
Corporate Structure
Business Address
Business Phone
Business Email
Business Alarm Code
Business Keys [*Location*]

Business Partner
Ownership Percentage
Phone
Email
Notes

Business Partner
Ownership Percentage
Phone
Email
Notes

Key Employee
Phone
Email
Notes

Key Employee
Phone
Email
Notes

Business Ownership
Important Business Documents

Important Business Documents

Name	Yes, I have	No, I don't have	Location
Buy-Sell Agreement			
Corporate Agreement			
Business Succession Plan			
Non-Disclosure Agreement			
Non-Solicitation Agreement			
Employee Handbook			
Key Employee Planning			
Employee Benefits			
Client Contracts			
Vendor Purchase Orders			
Health Insurance			
Life Insurance			
Disability Insurance			
Long Term Care Insurance			
Property and Casualty Insurance			
Tax Returns			
Bookkeeping Records			
Photos of Business Assets			
Asset Inventory			

Notes

Business Ownership

Important Business Documents

Cash Located at Business
Estimated Amount
Safe at Business
Key or Code
Key Location
Location of Safe
Who else has code or key?
Photos of contents in the safe   ◯ yes   ◯ no

Attach Inventory List

Notes

Document Originals & Copies

Document Name	Original/Copy	Document Location (Attached, Unknown, or N/A)
Birth Certificate(s)		
Driver's License(s)		
Marriage License		
Divorce/Separation Papers		
Health Insurance Card(s)		
Organ Donor Card(s)		
Record of Immunizations		
Record of Allergies		
Record of Disability		
Dental Records		
Child Identity Cards(s)		
DNA Swabs(s)		
Death Certificates		
Social Security Card(s)		
Passport/Green Card(s)		
Adoption Document(s)		
Mortgage or Real Estate Deed(s)		
Vehicle Registration(s)		
Family Tree		
Family Photograph(s)		
Prenuptial Document(s)		
Military Discharge Form (DD-214)		
Stocks/Bond Certificate(s)		
Frequent Flyer Mileage		
Reward Program List		
Location of Tax Returns		
Copy of Contents in Wallet		
Photos of All Personal Property		
Personal Property Appraisal(s)		
Home Inventory		
Firearm License		

Document Originals & Copies

Document Name	Original/Copy	Document Location (Attached, Unknown, or N/A)
Employment Contract(s)		
Cemetery Plot Deed(s)		
Second Set of Key(s)		
Time Share Agreement(s)		
Address Book		
Other		

Four-Legged Friends

Four-Legged Friends

Pet Information

Pet Information

Breed of Pet

Name of Pet

Birthdate

Person to care for this animal due to illness/accident

Person to take this animal upon my death

Type of Food

Type of Treats

Feeding Schedule

Medication(s)

Health History

Veterinarian

Veterinarian's Phone

Breeder

Breeder's Phone

License/Registration

Kennel

Additional Information (training, bed, habits)

Four-Legged Friends

Livestock Information

Livestock Information

Type of Livestock

Person to care for livestock due to illness/accident

Person to take livestock upon death

Type of Feed

Feeding Schedule

Medication(s)

Veterinarian

Veterinarian's Phone

Breeder

Breeder's Phone

Registered Papers

Person to notify to sell my livestock

Phone

Market Value

Additional Information

Estate Planning Documents

Estate Planning Documents

Estate Plan Information

Myself

My Name

Estate Planning Attorney's Name

Estate Planning Attorney's Phone

_____ Please initial here if you created your own estate planning documents.

I have a Will and/or Trust ○ yes ○ no

Location of this Document

Notes

I have Beneficiary Designations ○ yes ○ no

Location of this Document

Notes

I have an Advanced Care Directive ○ yes ○ no

Location of this Document

Notes

I have a Financial Durable Power of Attorney ○ yes ○ no

Location of this Document

Notes

I have a HIPAA Authorization ○ yes ○ no

Location of this Document

Notes

Special Instructions:

Estate Planning Documents

Estate Plan Information

Spouse/Partner

Spouse/Partner _____

Estate Planning Attorney's Name _____

Estate Planning Attorney's Phone _____

_____ Please initial here if you created your own estate planning documents.

I have a Will and/or Trust   ◯ yes ◯ no

Location of this Document _____

Notes

I have Beneficiary Designations   ◯ yes ◯ no

Location of this Document _____

Notes

I have an Advanced Care Directive   ◯ yes ◯ no

Location of this Document _____

Notes

I have a Financial Durable Power of Attorney   ◯ yes ◯ no

Location of this Document _____

Notes

I have a HIPAA Authorization   ◯ yes ◯ no

Location of this Document _____

Notes

Special Instructions:

Any important notes to this section:

Funeral Arrangements

Funeral Arrangements

Funeral Home & Cemetery Information

Myself

My Name

Family/Friend(s) making all final arrangements

Name

Phone

Name

Phone

Funeral Home

Funeral Director

Address

Phone

Notes

Cemetery

Contact Person

Address

Phone

Notes

Cemetery Plot ○ yes ○ no

Pre-paid Arrangements ○ yes ○ no

Location of Documents

Type of Casket

Details of Monument/Headstone

Instructions

Funeral Arrangements

Cemetery Information & Organ Donation

Myself

Embalm My Body ○ yes ○ no
Cremation ○ yes ○ no
Pre-paid Arrangements ○ yes ○ no
Location of Documents _____
Instructions
_____

○ Vault ○ Mausoleum *(Choose One)*
Pre-paid Arrangements ○ yes ○ no
Location of Documents _____
Type of Casket _____
Details of Monument/Headstone _____
Instructions
_____

Organ Donation ○ yes ○ no
Donor Card ○ yes ○ no
Organization _____
Address _____
Phone _____
Whole Body ○ yes ○ no
Only Specific Parts _____
Instructions
_____

Funeral Arrangements

Obituary

Myself

Publish Obituary ○ yes ○ no

I have written my obituary ○ yes ○ no
    If yes, included in binder

Include photograph in obituary ○ yes ○ no
    If yes, included in binder

I have not written my obituary (details to include)

Date and Place of Birth

Spouse/Partner/Significant Other

Children/Family

Education

Citizenship

Military Service

Occupations

Memberships/Hobbies

Volunteer

Achievements

Predeceased by

Flowers sent to

Donations sent to

Additional Thoughts

Publish obituary in the following locations:

Funeral Arrangements

Funeral Service Details

Myself

Service Location

Name _____
Contact Person _____
Address _____
Phone _____
Specific Details _____

Minister

Name _____
Contact Person _____
Address _____
Phone _____
Notes _____

Person to Deliver Eulogy

Name _____
Phone _____

Reading(s)/Poem(s)

Person to Read _____
Phone _____
Notes _____

Music/Hymns/Pianist/Vocalist

Name _____
Phone _____

Speaker(s)

Name _____
Phone _____

Funeral Arrangements

Funeral Service Details

Myself

Clothing or jewlery to be worn

Notes

Special items to be placed with body

Notes

Flower Arrangements

Notes

Instead of flowers, I would like donations made to

Photo Album or Pictures

Notes

Special Traditions

Notes

Memorial Cards

Notes

Grave Site Transportation

Notes

Funeral Arrangements

Funeral Service Details

Myself

Recommended Pallbearers

Name
Phone
Email

Name
Phone
Email

Name
Phone
Email

Name
Phone
Email

Name
Phone
Email

Name
Phone
Email

○ Open ○ Closed Casket   (Choose One)

Funeral Arrangements

Funeral Service Details

Myself

List of family/friends to invite to the service

Name
Phone
Email

Name
Phone
Email

Name
Phone
Email

Name
Phone
Email

Name
Phone
Email

Name
Phone
Email

Name
Phone
Email

Name
Phone
Email

Funeral Arrangements

Funeral Service Details

Myself

Reception Details

Location

Contact Person

Address

Phone

Date/Time

Food

Drinks

Notes

Funeral Arrangements

Funeral Home & Cemetery Information

Spouse/Partner

Spouse/Partner Name

Family/Friend(s) making all final arrangements

Name

Phone

Name

Phone

Funeral Home

Funeral Director

Address

Phone

Notes

Cemetery

Contact Person

Address

Phone

Notes

Cemetery Plot ○ yes ○ no

Pre-paid Arrangements ○ yes ○ no

Location of Documents

Type of Casket

Details of Monument/Headstone

Instructions

Funeral Arrangements

Cemetery Information & Organ Donation

Spouse/Partner

Embalm My Body   ○ yes ○ no
Cremation   ○ yes ○ no
Pre-paid Arrangements   ○ yes ○ no
Location of Documents _____
Instructions
[   ]

○ Vault ○ Mausoleums   *(Choose One)*
Pre-paid Arrangements   ○ yes ○ no
Location of Documents
Details of Monument/Headstone _____
Instructions
[   ]

Organ Donation   ○ yes ○ no
Donor Card   ○ yes ○ no
Organization _____
Address _____
Phone _____
Whole Body   ○ yes ○ no
Only Specific Parts _____
Instructions
[   ]

Funeral Arrangements

Obituary

Spouse/Partner

Publish Obituary ○ yes ○ no

I have written my obituary ○ yes ○ no
    If yes, included in binder

Include photograph in obituary ○ yes ○ no
    If yes, included in binder

I have not written my obituary (details to include)

Date and Place of Birth

Spouse/Partner/Significant Other

Children/Family

Education

Citizenship

Military Service

Occupations

Memberships/Hobbies

Volunteer

Achievements

Predeceased by

Flowers sent to

Donations sent to

Additional Thoughts

Publish obituary in the following locations:

Funeral Arrangements

Funeral Service Details

Spouse/Partner

Service Location
Name
Contact Person
Address
Phone
Specific Details

Minister
Name
Contact Person
Address
Phone
Notes

Person to Deliver Eulogy
Name
Phone

Reading(s)/Poem(s)
Person to Read
Phone
Notes

Music/Hymns/Pianist/Vocalist
Name
Phone

Speaker(s)
Name
Phone

Funeral Arrangements

Funeral Service Details

Spouse/Partner

Clothing or jewlery to be worn

Notes

Special items to be placed with body

Notes

Flower Arrangements

Notes

Instead of flowers, I would like donations made to

Photo Album or Pictures

Notes

Special Traditions

Notes

Memorial Cards

Notes

Grave Site Transportation

Notes

Funeral Arrangements

Funeral Service Details

Spouse/Partner

Recommended Pallbearers

Name
Phone
Email

Name
Phone
Email

Name
Phone
Email

Name
Phone
Email

Name
Phone
Email

Name
Phone
Email

○ Open ○ Closed Casket   *(Choose One)*

Funeral Arrangements

Funeral Service Details

Spouse/Partner

List of family/friends to invite to the service

Name
Phone
Email

Name
Phone
Email

Name
Phone
Email

Name
Phone
Email

Name
Phone
Email

Name
Phone
Email

Name
Phone
Email

Name
Phone
Email

Funeral Arrangements

Funeral Service Details

Spouse/Partner

Reception Details

Location

Contact Person

Address

Phone

Date/Time

Food

Drinks

Notes

Letters to Loved Ones

Letters to Loved Ones

This is a place to insert letters for the special people in your life.

Letters to Loved Ones

This is a place to insert letters for the special people in your life.

ABOOKS

ALIVE Book Publishing and ALIVE Publishing Group
are imprints of Advanced Publishing LLC,
3200 A Danville Blvd., Suite 204, Alamo, California 94507

Telephone: 925.837.7303 Fax: 925.837.6951
www.alivebookpublishing.com

www.ingramcontent.com/pod-product-compliance
Lightning Source LLC
Chambersburg PA
CBHW081923170426
43200CB00014B/2815